anythink

D0788026

Start TO finish
Second Series

FROM Joey TO Kangaroo

LISA OWINGS

LERNER PUBLICATIONS Minneapolis

Lerner Publications Company
A division of Lerner Publishing Group, Inc.
241 First Avenue North
Minneapolis, MN 55401 USA

For reading levels and more information, look up this title at www.lernerbooks.com.

Library of Congress Cataloging-in-Publication Data

The Cataloging-in-Publication Data for *From Joey to Kangaroo* is on file at the Library of Congress.
ISBN 978-1-5124-1830-9 (lib. bdg.)
ISBN 978-1-5124-1843-9 (pbk.)
ISBN 978-1-5124-1844-6 (EB pdf)

Manufactured in the United States of America
1-41174-23182-3/22/2016

TABLE OF Contents

Kangaroos are marsupials. How do they grow?

First, the mother kangaroo gets ready.

A mother kangaroo carries her baby for about one month. The baby is called a joey. When it is almost time to give birth, the mother cleans her pouch. The tiny joey will finish growing inside her pouch.

Then the joey is born.

The joey is only about the size of a jelly bean. It uses its **forelimbs** to climb into its mother's pouch. If the joey falls, its mother will not be able to help. It must reach the safety of her pouch alone.

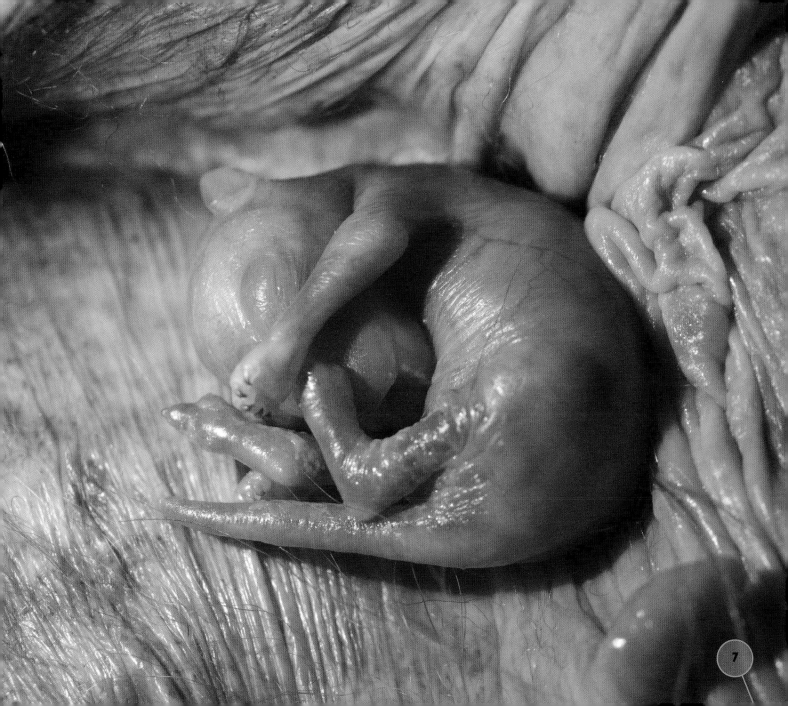

7

Next, the joey latches onto her teat.

Safe inside the pouch, the joey latches onto one of its mother's teats and drinks her milk. It stays permanently attached to the teat for the next several months.

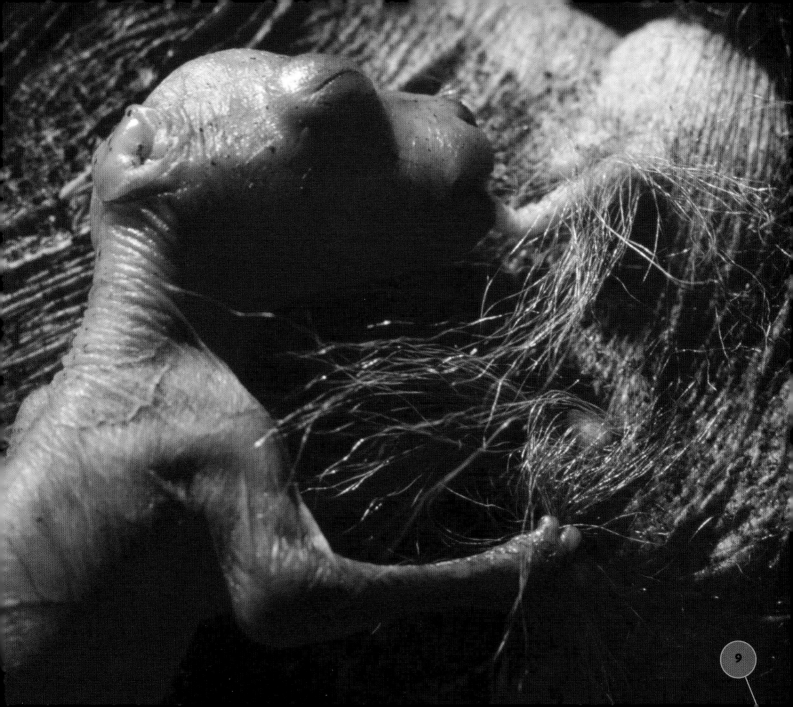

The joey grows inside the pouch.

The joey continues to develop inside the pouch. Its brain and body **mature**, and it sprouts fur. The pouch stays closed during this time to protect the joey.

Then it begins to explore its world.

After those first few months, the joey is ready to greet the world. Its mother lets it out for just minutes at first. Over time, she allows her joey out for longer periods to test its legs.

Soon the joey stops using the pouch.

The joey hops in and out of its mother's pouch. It dives in headfirst when it is scared, hungry, or tired. When the joey is between seven and ten months old, its mother stops letting it back in the pouch.

The joey still stays close to its mother.

The older joey no longer needs its mother's milk or the safety of her pouch. But the joey stays close, learning to search for grasses and other plants to eat. It also needs protection from other animals.

Finally, the kangaroo is fully grown.

Most kangaroos are full grown by two years old. Some males don't mature until the age of four. Kangaroos can weigh up to 200 pounds (90 kilograms). Females stay with their family group, but males leave their mothers.

It is ready to start its own family!

Young males begin to fight over and **mate** with females. Female kangaroos will **nurture** about three joeys every two years. They often have one out of the pouch, one in the pouch, and one on the way!

Glossary

forelimbs: limbs on the front of the body, where a human's arms would be. Joeys use their forelimbs for climbing and balance.

marsupials: animals that carry their young in a pouch on their bellies

mate: to join together to produce young

mature: to become fully developed or formed

nurture: to help something grow and develop

teat: the part of a mother mammal through which her young suckles milk

further Information

Donohue, Moira Rose. *Kangaroo to the Rescue! And More True Stories of Amazing Animal Heroes.* Washington, DC: National Geographic, 2015. Read about heroic kangaroos and enjoy other true animal tales.

Kids' Planet: Kangaroo
http://www.kidsplanet.org/factsheets/kangaroo.html
Check out this fact sheet about different types of kangaroos.

National Geographic Kids: Kangaroo
http://kids.nationalgeographic.com/animals/kangaroo/#kangaroo
-hopping.jpg
Dive into facts and photos about kangaroos.

Posada, Mia. *Who Was Here? Discovering Wild Animal Tracks.* Minneapolis: Millbrook Press, 2014. Track down and learn about kangaroos and other animals.

San Diego Zoo Kids: Aussie Animals Are Awesome!
http://kids.sandiegozoo.org/awesome_australia
Curious about other Australian animals? Visit this site to learn about koalas, echidnas, and more.

Index

Photo Acknowledgments
The images in this book are used with the permission of: © LifetimeStock/Shutterstock.com, p. 1; © Anan Kaewkhammul/Shutterstock.com, p. 3; © imageBROKER/Alamy, p. 5; © Ardea/Downer, Steve/Animals Animals, p. 7; Mitsuaki Iwago/Minden/Newscom, p. 9; © Katarina Christenson/Shutterstock.com, p. 11; © MasPix/Alamy, p. 13; © K.A. Willis/Shutterstock.com, p. 15; © FLPA/Alamy, p. 17; © Ingo Oeland/Alamy, p. 19; © iStockphoto.com/MaXpdia, p. 21.

Front cover: © Gerry Pearce /Alamy.

Main body text set in Arta Std Book 20/26.
Typeface provided by International Typeface Corp.

LERNER
e
SOURCE

Expand learning beyond the printed book. Download free, complementary educational resources for this book from our website, www.lerneresource.com.